34

Everyday History

Going to School

Philip Steele

W

FRANKLIN WATTS

NEW YORK • LONDON • SYDNEY

© 2000 Franklin Watts

First published in Great Britain by
Franklin Watts
96 Leonard Street
London
EC2A 4XD

Franklin Watts Australia
14 Mars Road
Lane Cove
NSW 2066
Australia

ISBN: 0 7496 3633 5 (hbk)
ISBN: 0 7496 3773 0 (pbk)
Dewey Decimal Classification 371
A CIP catalogue record for this book is available from
the British Library

Printed in Malaysia

Planning and production by Discovery Books Limited
Editors: Gianna Williams, Samantha Armstrong
Design: Ian Winton
Art Director: Jonathan Hair
Illustrators: Mike White, Stefan Chabluk,
Pamela Goodchild

Photographs:
4 top Bill Leimbach/South American Pictures, 4 bottom
Hutchison Picture Library, 6 Ashmolean Museum/
Bridgeman Art Library, 7 R. Sheridan/Ancient Art &
Architecture Collection, 8 top Archivo Municipal de
Historia, Barcelona/Bridgeman Art Library, 8 bottom
R. Sheridan/Ancient Art & Architecture Collection,
10 & 11 top R. Sheridan/Ancient Art & Architecture
Collection, 11 bottom Bibliotheque Nationale, Paris/
Bridgeman Art Library, 12 & 13 Mary Evans Picture
Library, 14 top National Gallery, Scotland/Bridgeman
Art Library, 14 bottom Natural History Museum/
Bridgeman Art Library, 16 National Gallery/Bridgeman
Art Library, 17 Dreweatt Neate Fine Art Auctioneers/
Bridgeman Art Library, 18 top Bridgeman Art Library,
18 bottom Discovery Picture Library, 19 bottom Mary
Evans Picture Library, 20 top Discovery Picture Library,
20 bottom Jacob A. Riis/Hulton Getty Picture
Collection, 21 top Josef Mensing Gallery/Bridgeman Art
Library, 21 bottom Agnew & Sons, London/Bridgeman
Art Library, 23 Mary Evans Picture Library, 24 &
25 Discovery Picture Library, 26 Bernard Gerard/
Hutchison Picture Library, 28 Neil McAllister/Bruce
Coleman, 29 Discovery Picture Library.

Acknowledgements
Franklin Watts would like to thank Casio Electronics
and Queen's College, London for the loan of their
material.

Contents

Before writing

In Stone Age times, about 10,000 years ago, children didn't have to go to school. But they had a lot to learn.

Today children are taught in school and at home. This Brazilian fisherman shows his son how to make an anchor.

Learning to survive

They had to find out how to chip flints and turn them into tools and weapons. They had to learn how to build shelters and to hunt wild animals. They had to know which plants were useful and which were poisonous. Children knew that their lives depended on such skills.

Coming of age

In many tribes, children were separated from their families to learn secret religious teachings. When they had passed certain tests, they became full members of the tribe and were considered to be adults. These girls are taking part in a coming of age ceremony in Sierra Leone, Africa.

Important skills

Later, people learned how to grow crops and raise animals. Children were now taught how to sow and harvest plants, how to herd cattle or shear sheep for wool. Practical skills were passed down from mother and father to daughter and son. Older people in the tribe would also serve as teachers, telling tales about ancient battles or gods and goddesses.

A tribal elder passes on his wisdom by word of mouth.

Over the ages, humans discovered how to read and write and solve mathematical problems. There was more and more for children to learn about. It was time for them to go to school.

In ancient times

Writing began in western Asia about 5,500 years ago. The first schools were set up by the Sumerians. If you wanted to be a tax collector or work for the royal court, you had to go to school. Sumerian priests taught children writing, mathematics, astronomy, architecture and the art of government.

Egyptian schools

About 3,500 years ago in Ancient Egypt, only the royal family and the sons of nobles and important officials went to school. The school might be a room at a royal court, or part of a temple. Lessons took place in the morning, before the day became too hot. Pupils learned how to read and write and do sums. They had to copy out sentences and learn lists off by heart. They were beaten soundly for poor work.

Exercise books

In ancient Egypt broken bits of pottery were used as disposable exercise books. They also used wooden books like the one shown here. In Greece and Rome children practised writing on wooden blocks which were covered in wax. The words were scratched with a sharp point called a stylus. The wax could be smoothed over if you made a mistake.

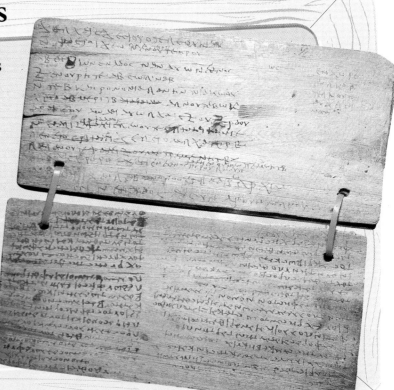

Greeks and Romans

By about 600BC, most Greek men
could read and write. In ancient
Greece, boys and girls began their
studies at the age of seven at private
schools. Boys were taught astronomy,
geometry, history, philosophy,
literature, sport and music. Girls were taught
reading, writing and arithmetic. By 300BC,
Roman schools were modelled on the Greek
system. Wealthy children were often taught
at home by a slave.

▲ Roman
children learned
to use pen and
ink as well as
the stylus.

Roman children
often had Greek
teachers.

Monks and scholars

Roman rule came to an end in Europe over 1,500 years ago. By then, most Europeans were Christians and monasteries provided most schooling.

Church schools

Poor country children had little hope of proper schooling, although some were taught to read by local priests or nuns. Larger towns had church schools. Boys of about seven to ten were taught the alphabet and singing.

▲ This picture of a monk teaching his pupils decorates a text that was hand-written about 600 years ago.

Royal approval

Medieval Europe was a place of warfare and unrest. Many kings had received little schooling. Luckily, a few wise rulers realised the importance of education. One was Charlemagne (AD742-814) who ruled most of France, Germany and northern Italy. Though he himself had difficulty reading and writing, he founded a school and a library at the royal court and encouraged the learning of Latin.

Learning letters

Printing was invented in China in the eighth century AD.
But there were no printed books in medieval Europe.
Pupils sitting in dark libraries had to copy out passages
from hand-written manuscripts, letter by letter.
They would try to make out the words in the Bible,
which was so valuable that it was kept on a chain.

The greatest centres of learning at this time
were in North Africa, Spain and the Middle
East, where Arab scholars studied
astronomy, mathematics
and geography.

An Arab scholar teaches
his pupils about the
constellations.

The new learning

By the 1400s, people in Europe had become more interested in learning about the world. They rediscovered the writing and art of the Ancient Greeks and Romans that seemed to have been forgotten. This new learning started in Italy and soon spread to other parts of Europe. The period became known as the Renaissance, which means 're-birth'

Students in the 1400s study law.

Merchant schools

Most teaching in Europe was still carried out by priests, monks and nuns. However in northern Europe, many people were rebelling against Catholic teachings. They were called Protestants and they closed down many of the old monasteries and churches. The schools attached to them often remained open, only now they were funded by rich merchants.

Apprentices

Merchants also funded the training of youngsters in practical skills such as metalworking and weaving. The trainees, called apprentices, would leave home to learn a skill in the house of the craftsman.

An apprentice is making thimbles in this workshop.

Books for schools

The new interest in learning happened at the same time as the arrival of printing in Europe. Printing was originally a Chinese invention, but during the 1440s new kinds of printing presses were set up in Germany and the Netherlands. Books no longer needed to be copied by hand. They could be printed over and over again and sold cheaply. Soon, textbooks were being printed for use in school classes.

Aztecs and Incas

In the 1500s, Europeans crossed the Atlantic Ocean to conquer Central and South America. They discovered great cities and schools to match those of many European towns.

Aztec schools

The Aztecs in Mexico had two types of school. Noble or very clever children were sent to a boarding school called a *calmecac*. There they learned history, law, mathematics, astronomy, religious studies, reading and writing. Girls learned weaving and embroidery.

Aztec symbols were usually written down on deerskin or bark.

Learning by heart

Most children went to the local day school, or *telpochcalli*. They studied farming skills, weapons training, history, public speaking, dancing and singing. Children had to learn facts by heart, singing and chanting while the teacher beat time.

Inca schools

The Spanish invaders found schools in Cuzco, at the centre of Peru's Inca empire. There was a school for noble children and the sons of chiefs who had been conquered. They learned mathematics and history, physical exercises and the Quechua language. After four years they took exams.

▲ The quipu was a frame of knotted cords used by the Incas for doing sums or keeping records.

Harsh punishments

Discipline was very strict in Aztec schools. Lazy boys would be pricked with cactus spines until they bled, or made to breathe in the smoke from burning chilli peppers. In Inca schools, bad behaviour was punished by caning on the soles of the feet.

Breathing the smoke from burning chilli peppers was an Aztec punishment.

Hornbooks and quills

By the 1600s in Europe, more and more boys – but still very few girls – were going to school. At the age of six or seven, many went to small grammar schools, so called because the main subject was Latin grammar. Schooling lasted for about seven years.

This Dutch school, painted in 1670, is an overcrowded, uncomfortable place.

A school day

School began at six in the morning and finished at four or five in the afternoon. Several classes could go on at once in the same room. Senior pupils helped out by teaching the youngest boys. The teacher's hand was never far from his birch cane.

Pens were cut from goose feathers using a pen-knife. They were dipped in the inkwell.

Children learned to read and write using a hornbook. This was a wooden board with a handle. Stuck on to it was a sheet of paper covered with letters, simple spellings or the Lord's Prayer. Children copied the words onto their slate. The paper was covered in transparent horn to protect it.

New World schools

In the 1600s Europeans were settling along the eastern coast of North America. The first grammar school was Boston's Latin School, which opened in 1635. America's first university, Harvard, was founded in 1636.

Make a hornbook

1 Cut a board and handle shape from stiff cardboard, as shown.

2 Write out a list of words you find difficult to spell on a sheet of paper. Paste the list onto the cardboard.

3 Tape a sheet of clear plastic over the paper and copy the words underneath onto a notebook.

Lessons at home

In the 1600s, it was common for the father to call all the family together to study the Bible, or to teach the children about right and wrong. When the father spoke, children were expected to remain silent. They spoke only when spoken to. Both the mother and father would help their children learn to read. Older children would be tested by reading aloud to the whole family. Still, by 1700, only one in three people in Europe could read.

Governesses

In the 1700s and 1800s, rich families often paid for a private teacher to visit or live in the family home. These tutors and governesses taught both girls and boys. Often the governesses were closer to the children than their own parents were.

A young governess teaches her pupil in the 1740s.

Private lessons

Private lessons still included Latin, Greek and arithmetic. Many children were now expected to learn French as well, which was spoken by important people all over Europe. Most children learned some history and geography. Girls would spend long hours practising needlework, watercolour painting, music and dancing.

Practice makes perfect

In the 1700s and 1800s girls had to practise their needlework on squares of cloth called samplers. They would embroider letters of the alphabet, family names, verses of poems, words from the Bible, designs of flowers or flags or pictures of their home. It was difficult work. If they made a mistake, they had to unpick their stitches until they were right.

The rich and the ragged

At the beginning of the nineteenth century schooling for most children was still basic or non-existent. Poor families were moving to the cities, searching for work. Their children were forced to work in mines and mills, or sweep chimneys. Some of these working children were given free lessons at 'ragged' schools by volunteer teachers.

This ragged school was in the Smithfield district of London.

Boarding Schools

Even wealthy children suffered at school. During the 1820s and 1830s, many of the grammar schools became boarding schools. Some offered a good education, but the worst were more like prisons.

Children were thrashed with straps and canes.

New ideas

However, times were changing. Firstly it was felt that the poor had the right to read the Bible. Then with the industrial revolution, people working in factories on complicated machinery needed to read, write and have technical training. By 1850, half the population of Europe could read and write.

One of the first colleges for girls, Queen's College, London was founded in 1848.

Compulsory schools

Schools were built in towns and countryside, and children had to go to them or break the law. Many girls' boarding schools, with women teachers, were founded. The first women were given university degrees in Oberlin, Ohio in 1841. By the 1870s, all teachers were properly trained and children were better cared for.

Dotheboys Hall

Some of the cheaper private boarding schools were terrifying places. Young boys were bullied and beaten. They received very little food and went for long periods without seeing their families. In 1838 the English writer Charles Dickens wrote about one of these schools, called Dotheboys Hall, in his famous book *Nicholas Nickleby*.

Slates and blackboards

Imagine you were going to school about 130 years ago. You might have to walk a long way to school, down muddy lanes. Boys wore jackets and breeches, and girls wore pinafores. Poor children had ragged clothes and some couldn't afford shoes. The start and end of lessons was marked by ringing a handbell.

An American class in the late 1890s salutes the flag.

The schoolroom

The classroom was heated by a stove and lit by oil or gas lamps. Wooden desks were lined up in rows. Young children practised writing or sums on slates. The teacher, often a woman, wrote on a blackboard, with chalk. Older children used lead pencils or steel-nibbed pens dipped in an inkwell.

The three Rs

Pupils spent long hours copying lessons out neatly in their exercise books. Most work involved the 'three Rs': reading, 'riting and 'rithmetic. Children had to learn lists of places or dates off by heart. If they were badly behaved, they had to stand in the corner, wearing a paper hat marked D (for 'dunce', a stupid person).

A naughty child is made to wear a dunce's cap.

In the playground

The school yard would be used for physical exercise each morning. The children did not wear special kit. They stood in lines while the teacher made them touch their toes or stretch their arms. During their breaks from lessons, the children would play hopscotch, leapfrog or skipping with ropes.

New frontiers

Some children in the 1800s and 1900s found themselves in wild and remote places, far from cities and schools, from the American West and the Canadian prairies, to South America, Australia and New Zealand. Where traditional, native schools existed, the new arrivals replaced them with their own school system.

Pioneer schools

Many pioneers took their families with them, by ship, covered wagon or oxcart. Parents taught their children to read and write when there was time, but they were often busy clearing land and setting up home. When an area became settled and prosperous, pioneer communities built the two most important landmarks of their towns — the church and the schoolhouse.

An American prairie school teacher calls her pupils to class.

Missionary schools

European countries ruled lands in Africa and Asia in the 1800s and 1900s. They built European schools for the children who lived there. There were Christian missions, where local children were taught reading, writing, arithmetic and the language of their new rulers – French, English, Dutch or Portuguese. During the last 50 years, most of these countries have won back their freedom and, when possible, built new schools for their children.

Growing up in the outback

In the dry and dusty lands of Australia, known as the 'outback', settlers lived on sheep stations hundreds of kilometres away from any others. How could children go to school? One answer was for the teacher to travel around from one to another. Another was for teachers to send lessons by post. Some children were sent to board in town schools. Today, outback children can talk with their teachers over the radio, or use the Internet.

Between the wars

By the 1930s, most people in Europe and North America could read and write. At this time, many people were still very poor. But children in the 1930s were better dressed and fed than in the 1890s. Many schools began to provide milk or meals.

▲ American children in the 1930s took lunch to school in a lunch pail.

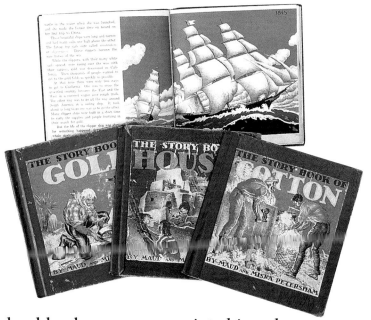

School books were now printed in colour.

Improving standards

Children now stayed at school longer, until they were 14 or perhaps 15 years old. More were able to read and write when they left, and secondary schools often included science laboratories, or halls for gymnastics. Discipline was still strict, and caning a threat that was often carried out.

There were new charts to help children learn to read.

School uniforms

Many schools made their pupils wear uniforms. In some schools, teachers wore a kind of uniform, too — a black gown and a tasselled cap called a mortarboard.

In many schools, the system of appointing student prefects, who made sure that rules were not broken, became widespread. Other children were given special jobs to do. The ink monitor gave out dip pens to the older children and made sure that the inkwells in their desks were filled each morning.

Prefects in an American school in the 1920s check that everyone's hands are clean

Design a school badge

1 Draw a picture that matches your school's name or its initials, or the school's activities like books and footballs.

2 Think of a motto for your school, and write it underneath the badge.

3 Copy out the badge on to stiff card and colour it in the school colours.

School can be fun!

In the 1950s, even young children still sat at classroom desks which were laid out in straight rows. Discipline was strict.

Colourful classrooms

During the 1960s, however, classrooms began to look brighter and more colourful. New school buildings were built with better facilities for indoor and outdoor activities. Children sat around tables and worked in small groups.

A cheerful classroom in the 1970s.

Relaxed environment

Instead of learning lists of facts, children were encouraged to find things out for themselves. Walls were covered with pupils' projects and paintings instead of dull maps and noticeboards. Schools became less strict. In many countries punishments such as beating were stopped and children no longer wore uniforms.

Television in schools

Schools television had been tried out in the United States as early as 1933. By the 1960s and 1970s educational programmes were being watched in many parts of the world.

Children from poorer backgrounds began to get the chance of a good education. In some parts of the world, like China and Russia, all children were now being educated for the first time.

No more sums?

From 1971, pocket calculators were available. Even the hardest sums could now be solved at the press of a button. School children were delighted. Why study arithmetic any more? Teachers weren't so enthusiastic. Some did allow calculators into the classroom, but said that children still had to use their brains as well!

A mouse in the class

If children from the 1400s could visit a classroom today, what would amaze them? They would see printed books on the shelves, have lessons about space and science, see boys and girls being treated as equals. They would be really astounded by computers.

Today children use sophisticated equipment to learn languages.

Computers

Computers can be used to find out information, to do projects in design and art, to write essays and stories and to play games. In the 1990s electronic whiteboards were developed. These allowed the teachers to work on a diagram, as they would on a normal whiteboard, but each pupil could interact with the same image on a personal computer monitor.

Information worldwide

Today the Internet is a worldwide network of computers linked by telephone. It allows children and schools all over the world to keep in touch with each other. It gives them access to libraries, newspaper articles and a huge variety of information sources.

The future

In future, will children simply use computers at home? Will teachers and classrooms exist? Let's hope so, because one important thing about learning was understood even by Stone Age hunters. Nothing can replace what we can learn from other people.

A substitute teacher?

Could a computer ever replace a teacher? There are already teaching programmes available on computer. They can provide information, set tasks, correct work and allocate marks. Computer graphics mean that learning could become more interactive and enjoyable. But how could a computer ever motivate a student to do better, or stop a student from simply switching to an electronic game?

Timeline

BC

c 3500	Sumerian schools are set up to teach writing.
c 2520	Reference to schools in Egypt.
c 600	Most male Greek citizens can read and write.
494	First written reference to schools in Greece.
c 200	Education and schools encouraged in China.

AD

117	Roman emperor Hadrian encourages the setting up of primary schools throughout the empire.
800	The Frankish ruler Charlemagne encourages schools and learning.
1500s	Schools in the Aztec empire of Mexico and the Inca empire of Peru.
1540	A printed class textbook is published in England - *Lily's Latin Grammar*.
1543	First state-funded schools, in Meissen and Saxony (Germany).
1635	Latin School founded in Boston, North America.
1647	A law passed in Massachustts, USA requires all towns to set up schools.
1684	Teacher training college opened in France.
1697	First Sunday schools open in Wales.
1837	First kindergarten set up in Switzerland.
1867	US Congress sets up a Bureau of Education.
1753	First cookery lesson in school held in Scotland.
1774	Science taught for the first time in London, England.
1870	All children in Britain required to to go to school until the age of 10.
1903	First school bus used in Paris, France.
1909	Italian Maria Montessori tries a method of replacing strict discipline with teaching that is enjoyable for children.
1924	Radio for schools set up in Great Britain.
1939-45	World War II. Education interrupted worldwide for millions of children.
1944	British school leaving age is now 15.
1949	Schools televison service begins in Philadelphia, USA.
1980s	Computers in school.

Glossary

Apprentice Someone who is learning a trade or craft.

Astronomy Study of the stars and the night sky.

Blackboard A large board painted black on which words can be written in chalk.

Constellations Stars that are grouped together to make them easier to recognise.

Flint A type of hard stone.

Governess A woman paid to look after the education of children within a family.

Grammar school A type of school, originally teaching Latin and Greek grammar.

Hornbook A wooden board covered in horn, holding reading exercises.

Inkwell A small pot used to hold ink.

Manuscript A text written out by hand.

Merchant Someone who makes his or her living by trading goods.

Mortarboard A black cap worn by teachers and sometimes by students.

Quill A pen cut from the horny point of a feather.

Quipu A system of knotted cords used by the Inca people of Peru as a kind of calculator.

Renaissance The re-birth of learning and the arts in Europe during the 1400s and 1500s.

Sampler A piece of cloth used to practice needlework skills.

Slate A small piece of flat stone which was used for writing.

Stylus A tool with a sharp point, used for writing on wax.

University A place where people carry out advanced studies or research after they have left school.

Whiteboard A white display board on which you can write with a felt-tip pen.

Further reading

Thomson, Ruth, *Changing Times: School*, Franklin Watts, 1994
Shuter, Jane, *School: Picture the Past series*, Heinemann Library, 1997
Stoppleman, Monica, *School Day: Turn of the Century series*, A&C Black, 1990
Wood, Richard: *A Victorian School*, Wayland, 1994

Index